RICK STEIN

FRESH FROM THE SEA

PENGUIN BOOKS

PENGUIN BOOKS

Published by the Penguin Group. Penguin Books Ltd, 27 Wrights Lane, London w8 5TZ, England. Penguin Books USA Inc., 375 Hudson Street, New York, New York 10014, USA. Penguin Books Australia Ltd, Ringwood, Victoria, Australia. Penguin Books Canada Ltd, 10 Alcorn Avenue, Toronto, Ontario, Canada M4V 3B2. Penguin Books (NZ) Ltd, 182–190 Wairau Road, Auckland 10, New Zealand · Penguin Books Ltd, Registered Offices: Harmondsworth, Middlesex, England · This selection is from *English Seafood Cookery* by Richard Stein. Published in Penguin Books 1988. This edition published 1996 · Copyright © Richard Stein, 1988. All rights reserved · Typeset by Rowland Phototypesetting Ltd, Bury St Edmunds, Suffolk. Printed in England by Clays Ltd, St Ives plc · Except in the United States of America, this book is sold subject to the condition that it shall not, by way of trade or otherwise, be lent, re-sold, hired out, or otherwise circulated without the publisher's prior consent in any form of binding or cover other than that in which it is published and without a similar condition including this condition being imposed on the subsequent purchaser · 10 9 8 7 6 5 4 3 2 1

CONTENTS

Soups, Starters and Salads   1

  Crab in Filo Pastry   3
  Cod and Mussel Chowder   4
  Velvet Crab and Chilli Soup   5
  Fish Soup   7
  Mussel and Leek Soup   9
  Mousseline of Finnan Haddock   10
  Marinated Herring with Cream   12
  Hot Potato Salad with Smoked Mackerel and Dandelions   13
  Marinated Salmon Trout   14
  Salmon Marinated in Fresh Lime Juice   15
  A Warm Salmon Salad   16
  A Wilted Salad of Scallops, Prawns and Mussels   17

Light Meals   21

  John Dory with Basil and Monbazillac   23
  Red Mullet with a Tomato and Tarragon Dressing   24
  Mussels with Tomato and Basil   25

Deep-fried Scallops Wrapped in Parma Ham	26
Sautéed Scallops with Mange-tout Peas	27

Main Courses   29

Lemon Sole in Puff Pastry	31
Seafood Thermidor	33
Fish Cakes with Turmeric, Coriander and Cardamom	35
Hake and Potato Pie	36
Leek and Hake Quiche	37
Baked Plaice with Cheese and Cider	38
Plaice and Artichoke Pie	39
Escalopes of Shark with Noisette Butter	40
A *Fricassée* of Skate with Mushrooms	42
Char-grilled Conger Eel with a Rich Red Wine Sauce	43
Cassolette of Brill, Scallops and Crab	45
Fillets of Brill *Dugléré*	46
Poached Halibut Steaks with Hollandaise Sauce	47
Monkfish Cooked Like a Gigot of Lamb	48
Poached Salmon with *Sauce Verte*	48

Basics   51

Fish Stock	53
Rouille	54

Cleaning Mussels 55
Velouté 56
Aïoli 57

Soups, Starters and Salads

CRAB IN FILO PASTRY WITH GINGER AND LIME

Frozen leaves of filo pastry in packets are quite easy to get hold of now. Filo pastry is ideal for wrapping round small morsels of seafood for a cocktail canapé. These quantities will make 24 canapés.

3 oz (90 g) white crab meat
½ teaspoon (2.5 ml) finely chopped fresh ginger
zest and juice of half a lime
½ oz (15 g) butter
tiny pinch of cayenne
2 leaves of filo pastry about 12 by 16 inches (30 by 40 cm)
melted butter for brushing the filo leaves

Mix the crab meat with the ginger, lime, butter and cayenne. Lay out the first leaf of filo and brush it with melted butter. Lay the second leaf on top and brush that with butter. Cut the leaves into squares with sides of 2½ inches (6.2 cm).

Set the oven at 425°F (220°C; gas mark 7).

Place a teaspoon of the crab mixture at the centre of each square and fold one corner over to the opposite corner to form a triangle. Squeeze the edges together. Put on a baking tray and bake in the oven for 6 to 8 minutes.

COD AND MUSSEL CHOWDER

The combination of fish, molluscs and salt pork in a cream-based soup is most agreeable. Fish stews made on this basis are as exciting in a Northern Atlantic way as the combination of fish, tomato, olive oil and garlic is in a Mediterranean stew like *bouillabaisse*.

20 mussels
2 oz (60 g) salt pork, cut into small dice
1 oz (30 g) butter
4 oz (120 g) onions, diced
8 oz (240 g) potatoes, diced and not washed
  (you need the starch to thicken the liquid)
10 fl oz (300 ml) milk
4 fl oz (120 ml) cream
1 bayleaf, sliced (preferably a fresh one)
the liquor from cooking the mussels
4 oz (120 g) cod fillet, skinned
a small amount of freshly chopped parsley
2 water biscuits

Clean the mussels and open them by placing them in a pan with a splash of water and steaming them over a high heat with a lid on the saucepan. As soon as the mussels open, take off the heat and drain them through a colander, saving the cooking liquor in a bowl underneath. When the mussels have cooled enough to handle, remove the meats from the shells and take out the beards.

Fry the diced pork in butter till beginning to brown, then add the onions and fry till soft.

At the same time, bring the potatoes to the boil in the milk and cream with the bayleaf. Slowly simmer till still firm but not raw. Add the pork and onions and the mussel juice and simmer for another five minutes. Season with salt if necessary and black pepper.

Add the cod fillet, cut into smallish pieces, and simmer till cooked, then add the mussels; do not continue to cook or you will toughen the mussels up. Pour the chowder into a serving tureen and finish with the chopped parsley and crushed water biscuits.

VELVET CRAB AND CHILLI SOUP

Velvet or swimming crabs are not well known in the British Isles, though plenty are caught in lobster and crab pots here. Most are exported to France and Spain, where they are highly esteemed. They are small, just a little bigger than the green shore crab, and therefore best turned into soups. They have an exquisite sweet fresh flavour, so if you are on holiday on the coast and see signs of lobster and crab fishing, ask around.

2 lb (900 g) velvet crabs
2 oz (60 g) red peppers without seeds

½ oz (15 g) green chillies without seeds
3 cloves of garlic, peeled and chopped
3 oz (90 g) onion, peeled and sliced
2 fl oz (60 ml) olive oil
1 teaspoon (5 ml) tomato purée
2 pints (1.2 litres) fish stock
1 oz (30 g) broken pasta

Drop the crabs into fiercely boiling water. Boil for a couple of minutes till all are dead. Remove the back shell from the crabs. Also remove the stomach sac, which is situated at the front of the body shell below the eyes; in making any bisque-type soup where you are going to liquidize the shell as well as everything else, it is a good idea to remove the stomach. Otherwise, if the shellfish has been feeding in a sandy or muddy area, the grit thus ingested will find its way through to the finished soup. Everything else can go in, however. Cut the crabs into 5 or 6 pieces. Chop the red pepper and chillies and put them in a saucepan with the garlic, onion and olive oil. Fry over a medium heat to bring out the flavour. Stir in the crabs and add the tomato purée, sweat for a further couple of minutes, then pour on the fish stock. Bring to the boil and simmer for 20 minutes.

Liquidize everything (do it in small amounts if your liquidizer isn't particularly robust). Pass the liquidized soup through a conical strainer, pushing it through with the back of the ladle. After passing it once through the conical strainer, pass it twice more through a fine sieve. Reheat the soup and add the pasta. Simmer till the pasta is cooked, then serve.

FISH SOUP

The sort of *soupe de poissons* that you find in virtually every coastal restaurant in France.

Now that almost everyone owns a liquidizer, a common error in making fish soup is to include the heads and bones of the fish when liquidizing. This gives the soup a bitter gluey flavour which one also notices too often in French restaurants.

In this recipe the fish is filleted first, and the stock, made with the bones, is strained and added with the fillets of fish. We always try to combine a mixture of fish with body, like conger or dogfish, with some cheap white fish like pollack or whiting, gurnard or grey mullet; and there is no reason why you shouldn't include in the initial fish stock any shellfish scraps you might have.

The quantities below make plenty of soup for four.

2–3 lb (900 g–1.3 kg) fish: conger eel, skate, cod, dogfish, shark – virtually any fish except oily ones like mackerel and herring
3 pints (1.7 litres) water
5 fl oz (150 ml) olive oil
6 oz (180 g) onion, peeled and roughly chopped

6 oz (180 g) celery, washed and roughly chopped
6 oz (180 g) leek, washed and roughly chopped
6 oz (180 g) Florence fennel, roughly chopped
5 cloves of garlic
a 2-inch (5-cm) piece of orange peel
10 oz (300 g) tomatoes
2 teaspoons (10 ml) tomato purée
a quarter of a large red pepper, blistered under the grill and peeled
1 bayleaf
a large pinch of saffron
salt and ground black pepper
a large pinch of cayenne pepper

Fillet all the fish and use the heads and bones to make a fish stock with the 3 pints (1.7 litres) of water.

Heat the olive oil in a large pan and add the onion, celery, leek, Florence fennel and garlic. Cook with a little colour till the vegetables are very soft (about 45 minutes). Add the orange peel, tomatoes, tomato purée, red pepper, bayleaf, saffron and the fish fillets. Cook briskly, turning everything over as you do. Now add the fish stock, bring to the boil and simmer for 40 minutes.

Liquidize the soup and pass it through a conical strainer, pushing as much as you can through with the back of a ladle. Put it back on the heat and heat up. Season with salt, pepper and cayenne. The soup should be a little on the salty side, with a subtle but noticeable heat about it from the cayenne.

Serve the soup with some French bread, thinly sliced and fried in olive oil, then rubbed with garlic, some grated cheese (Emmenthal or Parmesan) and some *rouille*. Spread the croutons with *rouille* and float them on the soup scattered with the cheese.

MUSSEL AND LEEK SOUP

Mussels and leeks go very well together to make, with saffron, a soup that smells and tastes quite exotic. Mussels are so abundant round our coastline that it is a pity they are not more readily available at fishmongers throughout Britain. It could be a question of demand creating a supply; so the more you ask for them, the better.

> *3 lb (1.4 kg) or 3 pints (1.7 litres) mussels*
> *1 fl oz (30 ml) white wine*
> *8 oz (240 g) leeks*
> *1 small onion*
> *3 oz (90 g) butter*
> *1½ oz (45 g) plain flour*
> *15 fl oz (450 ml) fish stock*
> *a good pinch of saffron*
> *2 fl oz (60 ml) double cream*

Thoroughly wash the mussels, scraping off barnacles and discarding any mussels that are gaping open and don't close up when given a good tap. Place the cleaned mussels in a pan. Add a dash of the wine, cover and cook over a high heat for about 5 minutes, shaking the pan until the mussels have opened. Strain the liquor through a colander into a bowl, shaking the colander well to drain off all the juice lodged in the shells.

Cut up the leeks and the onion. Melt the butter in a saucepan and soften the vegetables in it on a low heat for about 3 minutes. Add the remaining wine and let it reduce by half. Add the flour and stir until smooth. Mix the mussel liquor with the fish stock and gradually add it to the pan, stirring well. When the soup is smooth and simmering, add a good pinch of saffron and leave to cook for 25 minutes.

While it is simmering, pull all the beards out of the mussels and discard one half of each shell. Liquidize the soup and strain through a sieve into a clean saucepan. Reheat and stir in the cream and the mussels. Serve hot.

MOUSSELINE OF FINNAN HADDOCK WITH A HORSERADISH SAUCE

You can make this with lesser varieties of smoked haddock, but you can't beat the real thing.

1½ lb (700 g) Finnan haddock, weighed on the bone
1 egg and 1 egg yolk
½ oz (15 g) peeled onion
1 level teaspoon (5 ml) salt

juice of a quarter lemon
12 fl oz (360 ml) double cream

For the Horseradish Sauce

2 teaspoons (10 ml) freshly grated horseradish (or horseradish sauce if you can't get fresh)
2 fl oz (60 ml) double cream
½ teaspoon (2.5 ml) white wine vinegar (leave this out if using horseradish sauce)
pinch of salt

Ask your fishmonger to fillet and skin the Finnan haddock for you. Place the haddock, eggs, onion, salt and lemon juice in a food processor and blend until smooth. Pour in the cream, which must be well chilled, and continue to blend for 15 seconds only (don't go on any longer or you will curdle it). Chill the mixture for 30 minutes.

Set your oven to 300°F (150°C; gas mark 2).

Butter a suitable mould (I use a small bread tin about 9 by 4 by 2 inches, 23 by 10 by 5 cm), fill it with the mousseline and cover with buttered foil. Find a shallow tray in which you can fit your mould, place the mould in the tray and half fill the tray with water. Bring the water in the tray to the boil on top of the cooker and then transfer to the top shelf of the oven and cook for about 40 minutes. To test if the mousseline is cooked, insert a trussing needle or thin knife into the centre and test on your top lip; if it feels warm the mousseline is cooked enough. Remove from the oven, leave to cook and chill for at least 4 hours.

Turn out the mousseline by dipping the mould in a sink full of hot water while you count to six, then invert over a tray, bringing the mould down with a sharp tap. Make the horseradish sauce by mixing all the ingredients, and serve a slice of mousseline with a spoonful of sauce.

MARINATED HERRING WITH CREAM

Somewhat similar to soused herring but far superior.

4 fl oz (120 g) white wine vinegar
½ pint (300 ml) water
2 teaspoons (10 ml) sugar
1 teaspoon (5 ml) salt
12 black peppercorns
2 bayleaves
sprig of thyme
2 herrings, each weighing 6–8 oz (180–240 g)
3 tablespoons (45 ml) cream
2 thin pieces of lemon peel
1 small onion, peeled and sliced

Put all the ingredients except the herrings, cream, lemon peel and onion in a saucepan. Boil, then simmer for 15 minutes and leave to cool.

Fillet the herrings and place the herring fillets in a shallow dish. Just cover them with the marinade, topping up with a little water if necessary. Bring this up to the boil, let it bubble once, then immediately take it off the heat.

Mix the cream with 3 tablespoons (45 ml) of the cold marinade and pour on to 4 plates. Place a fillet on each. Cut the lemon peel into very fine strips and put two strips on each fillet with some onion. Serve cold with brown bread and butter.

HOT POTATO SALAD WITH SMOKED MACKEREL AND DANDELIONS

The bitterness of the dandelions goes very well with the smoke in the mackerel. There is something very satisfying about using weeds to flavour a dish.

10 oz (300 g) new potatoes
1 oz (30 g) dandelion leaves
½ oz (15 g) finely chopped onion
3 oz (90 g) smoked mackerel
3 fl oz (90 ml) basic dressing

Scrub the potatoes and boil them. Wash the dandelion leaves and pull away the stems. Blanch the leaves in boiling water for a few seconds, then refresh them in cold water. Drain them in a sieve. Chop the onion. Remove skin and bone from the mackerel and cut into slices 1 by ¼ inch (2.5 cm by 6 mm). Slice the potatoes into ¼-inch (6-mm) slices and place in a saucepan with the dandelion leaves and onions, add the dressing, and warm everything through. Put the salad into a bowl and serve with a few turns of your black pepper-mill.

MARINATED SALMON TROUT WITH LIME AND GINGER

Thinly sliced salmon trout marinated in a dressing made with ginger, fresh lime juice and pink peppercorns. If you can't get hold of pink peppercorns leave them out, but they are available nowadays in good delicatessens. It is quite hard to slice raw salmon trout very thinly, but if you do the best you can, sandwich the slices between two plates, and apply a little gentle pressure, you will find the results quite passable.

8 oz (240 g) salmon trout fillet, free from bones

The Dressing

4 fl oz (120 ml) groundnut oil
¼ oz (7.5 g) fresh ginger, peeled and finely chopped
1 teaspoon (5 ml) of pink peppercorns
juice and zest of one lime
½ teaspoon (2.5 ml) salt

Place the fillet, skin side down, on a chopping board. Take a very sharp thin-bladed knife and cut thin slices, cutting on the slant towards the tail as you would slice smoked salmon. Cut enough to cover 4 dinner plates. Flatten the fish if necessary by pressing a clean plate down on to the slices, cover with clingfilm and refrigerate until just before you want to serve the fish. As slicing the fish is quite tricky it is a good idea to do it some time in advance.

Make the dressing by combining all the ingredients.

Five minutes before serving, put the dressing on the fish, spreading it over with the back of a teaspoon.

SALMON MARINATED IN FRESH LIME JUICE WITH A CHIVE MAYONNAISE

The less you have to cook salmon and salmon trout, the better it tastes; so when the slices of salmon are 'cooked' for only five minutes in fresh lime juice one can't do much better than to eat it absolutely raw like the Japanese. The idea of cooking fish in citrus juice is common in Caribbean cookery.

For this recipe, follow exactly the same instructions for the salmon trout (p. 14) but five minutes before serving squeeze the juice of a lime on each plate of salmon, rub it around with the back of a spoon and sprinkle it with a very little salt. Serve with mayonnaise, to which you should add a little double cream and some freshly chopped chives.

A WARM SALMON SALAD

This is the sort of dish I love in the early summer: an uncomplicated way of presenting some fresh salmon. For a change I have included salad ingredients that you can readily buy. But naturally I would use a variety of different types of lettuce and probably some sorrel, cress grown outside, and some young rocket too.

> *a 1-lb (450-g) piece of salmon on the bone*
> *salt and freshly ground black pepper*
> *½ teaspoon (2.5 ml) fresh chopped tarragon*
> *1 lettuce*
> *1 bunch of watercress*
> *1 bunch of spring onions*
> *3 fl oz (90 ml) olive oil dressing*

Set your oven to 300°F (150°C; gas mark 2).

Take a piece of aluminium foil about 12 inches (30 cm) square and brush it with olive oil. Brush the piece of salmon with oil, season well, and sprinkle it with chopped tarragon. Parcel the salmon up loosely in the foil by folding one half over the other and turning over the edges. Place the parcel on a baking tray and bake gently in the slow oven for about 45 minutes until just cooked. It should be slightly undercooked in the middle (a darker shade of pink).

Meanwhile prepare the salad. Wash the lettuce and dry it. Remove the thickest watercress stalks and the outer skins of the spring onions. Cut the white of the spring onions from the green and slice the white part diagonally. Put in a bowl with the lettuce and cress and toss with half of the olive oil dressing.

Chop the green part of the spring onions into ⅛-inch (3-mm) pieces and put in a small saucepan with the rest of the dressing.

When the salmon is cooked, unwrap it and pour the cooking juices into the saucepan with the chopped spring onion and dressing. Remove the skin and bones from the salmon, break the fillet into pieces and arrange over the salad. Warm the dressing in the saucepan through and pour over the warm salmon; serve at once.

You can make a main course of this dish by using a 1½-lb (700-g) piece of salmon and adding some new potatoes boiled with mint.

A WILTED SALAD OF SCALLOPS, PRAWNS AND MUSSELS

A seafood salad which is slightly warmed up under the grill so that the leaves go limp. Salad leaves treated in this way taste totally different. By increasing the quantities, this will make a very pleasant main course.

4 scallops
20 mussels

1 courgette
salad leaves for 4 people (as varied as possible, e.g. lettuce, spinach, rocket, sorrel and a few dandelion leaves)
2 fl oz (60 ml) olive oil dressing
2 good-sized tomatoes, peeled, deseeded and chopped
½ oz (15 g) onion, finely chopped
5 leaves of basil
20 shelled prawns

Clean the scallops and slice each one into three. Brush a small grilling tray with a little oil and brush the scallops. 'Set' the scallops under the grill (i.e. cook them only enough to firm them up). Remove and cool down.

Clean the mussels, then open them in a pan with the lid on over a high heat. Strain through a colander; keep the cooking liquor for another dish. Shell and remove the beards from the mussels.

Cut the courgette into julienne strips, ⅛ by ⅛ by 1¾ inches (3 mm by 3 mm by 4.5 cm).

Toss the salad leaves in a bowl with half the olive oil dressing and the courgette strips.

Mix tomato, onion, the rest of the olive oil dressing and the basil (which should be roughly chopped) in a small saucepan. Add the scallops, mussels and prawns. Warm this through, but do not let it get hot.

Turn on your overhead grill.

Place salad leaves on 4 plates and arrange the scallops,

mussels, prawns and the tomato and basil dressing on top.

Finally place the 4 salads under your grill for only enough time to wilt the salad leaves – about 20 seconds. Serve immediately.

Light Meals

JOHN DORY WITH BASIL AND MONBAZILLAC

Monbazillac is like Sauternes and goes exceptionally well with chopped basil in a cream-based sauce.

> *four 2½–3-oz (75–90-g) fillets of John Dory, or*
> *   4 small fish each weighing 6–8 oz (180–240 g)*
> *butter for grilling*
> *salt and freshly ground pepper*
> *½ pint (300 ml) fish stock*
> *1 fl oz (30 ml) Monbazillac (or Sauternes, or*
> *   perhaps Muscat de Beaumes de Venise)*
> *3 fl oz (90 ml) double cream*
> *10 basil leaves*

Turn on your overhead grill. Butter a shallow grilling tray and place the fillets on it, skin side down. Butter and lightly season them. Place the fish stock and wine in a small pan and reduce by three-quarters. Add the cream and reduce by rapid boiling until the sauce coats the back of a spoon. Add the basil and serve.

RED MULLET WITH A TOMATO AND TARRAGON DRESSING

We often have this dish on the menu at the restaurant, but for some reason it doesn't sell very well. This is a great pity, because it is a treat too good to be missed.

It is usual to cook red mullet with the liver left in, because it adds immeasurably to the flavour of the fish. Even if I am cooking a dish of fillets of red mullet I try to put the liver in somewhere.

4 small red mullet, each weighing about 6–7 oz (180–210 g)

For the Dressing

3 good-sized tomatoes, peeled, deseeded and chopped
1 teaspoon (5 ml) chopped fresh tarragon
1 shallot or half a small onion, very finely chopped
3 fl oz (90 ml) olive oil
1 tablespoon (15 ml) fresh lemon juice
salt and freshly ground black pepper

Scale and remove the fins from the mullet. Make a small incision in the belly and remove the gut, but not the liver. Turn on your overhead grill.

Brush the grilling tray with a little olive oil and place the fish on it. Season them with salt and ground black pepper and grill. Being a dense fish, they may take longer than you expect: about 4 minutes a side for fish this small. While they are grilling, mix together the dressing ingredients and warm through in a small saucepan; don't let it get too hot.

Lay the fish on warm plates, put the sauce beside and decorate each plate with a tarragon leaf.

MUSSELS WITH TOMATO AND BASIL

> 50 to 60 good-sized mussels (more if you can only get small ones)
> a splash of white wine
> 1 oz (30 g) finely chopped shallot or onion
> 1 fl oz (30 ml) olive oil
> 6 oz (180 g) tomato, peeled, deseeded and chopped
> 3 cloves of garlic, finely chopped
> 8 basil leaves
> 1 teaspoon (5 ml) chopped parsley

Clean the mussels and put them in a large saucepan on a fierce heat. Sprinkle in some white wine, put a lid on and cook till the mussels open. Remove from the heat as soon as they have opened, strain off the liquor and keep it. Remove the beards from the mussels and discard one half of each shell. Set the mussels in the half shells on a dish.

Soften the shallots in the olive oil over a moderate heat and add about 3 fl oz (90 ml) of the mussel cooking liquor (keep the rest for other dishes: for example, add some to fish stock to improve its flavour). Reduce the mussel liquor down till it has almost disappeared, then add the tomatoes, heat through and add the garlic. Warm through again to drive off some but not all of the volatility of the garlic, then add the basil freshly snipped up with a pair of scissors in a glass (this passes as much as possible of the ephemeral basil flavour into the dish). Add the parsley and season the sauce with salt and ground black pepper.

Heat the mussels through in the oven; don't overdo it or they will toughen up. Spoon the sauce into the mussel shells and serve.

DEEP-FRIED SCALLOPS WRAPPED IN PARMA HAM

Most frozen scallops have been soaked in water before freezing, so that they swell up to about twice their natural size, which rather spoils their flavour. But you can sometimes get them quite cheap, and this recipe, though it would not be the right treatment for perfectly fresh scallops, turns the frozen variety into something extremely pleasant to eat.

You could also use this recipe for scallop-shaped pieces of cod or monkfish.

8 scallops
4 oz (120 g) Parma ham (or any other very thin-sliced ham)

2 oz (60 g) flour
2 eggs
2 oz (60 g) fresh breadcrumbs
tartare sauce

Cut each scallop in half, and roll each half in a piece of Parma ham. Put the flour in one small tray; whisk the eggs and put them in a second tray; put the breadcrumbs in a third, and pass the scallops through the flour, then the egg, then the breadcrumbs. A small tip on how to do this – probably obvious to you, but it took me some time to think of it – put all the scallops in the flour, then all in the egg, then all in the breadcrumbs. (I used to do them one at a time and got in an awful mess, with the egg everywhere.) Deep-fry until golden brown (about 2 minutes). Serve with homemade tartare sauce.

SAUTÉED SCALLOPS WITH MANGE-TOUT PEAS

Very much a dish for perfectly fresh scallops. They are just seared in a very hot pan, so that you get the best of both worlds, the sweet caramelized taste of fried scallops on the outside and with the delicacy of undercooked scallops as well.

4 oz (120 g) mange-tout peas
8 scallops
1 oz (30 g) unsalted butter

1 teaspoon (5 ml) chopped parsley
salt and ground black pepper

Wash, top and tail the mange-tout peas and blanch them in boiling salted water for 2 minutes. Drain and refresh in cold water.

Cut the scallops into 3 slices. Take a thick-bottomed frying pan and heat until extremely hot. Put in a small knob of the butter, quickly brush it around the bottom of the pan with a pastry brush, and immediately throw in the scallops. Cook for about 10 seconds and turn over with a palette knife or toss. Cook for a further 20 seconds, take off the heat and lift the scallops out with a fish slice into a warm dish.

Put in the rest of the butter and then the mange-tout peas and the parsley. Return to the heat and let the peas warm through in the butter. Season with salt and black pepper. Add the peas, parsley and cooking butter to the warm scallops and serve.

Main Courses

LEMON SOLE IN PUFF PASTRY WITH CIDER, MUSHROOMS AND CREAM

The filling for this puff pastry *tourte* is not baked with the pastry; the two are combined just before serving so that the crust stays crisp and light.

> *1 large lemon sole, about 1½ lb (720 g)*
> *1 lb (450 g) puff pastry, butter or frozen*
> *1 egg (for egg wash)*
> *2 oz (60 g) onion, finely chopped*
> *½ teaspoon (2.5 ml) salt*
> *3 fl oz (90 ml) dry cider*
> *4 oz (120 g) fresh white button mushrooms, thinly sliced*
> *4 fl oz (120 ml) double cream*
> *10 fl oz (300 ml) fish velouté*
> *cayenne pepper and lemon juice*

Turn on the oven at 450°F (230°C; gas mark 8).

Remove the four fillets from the lemon sole. Skin them and cut each in two. Make a fish stock with the bones, using a pint (600 ml) of water and about 10 oz (300 g) vegetables.

Roll out the puff pastry on a lightly floured surface till it is a quarter inch (6 mm) thick. Cut out a circle 12 inches (30 cm) in diameter, then place a 10-inch (25.5-cm) dinner plate on the pastry and gently cut a circle round it, halfway through the pastry. Put the pastry on a suitable baking sheet and rest it in the refrigerator for 10 minutes. Break the egg, whisk it up with a fork and brush the top of the pastry with it, using a pastry brush. Bake for about 12 minutes until golden brown and nicely risen.

Butter a shallow pan and place the onion then the fish fillets in it. Season with salt and pour on the cider. Cover with a butter paper and cook gently on the top of the stove until the fish has just turned white.

Cook the sliced mushrooms gently in a little butter.

Cut the top from the baked puff pastry (this will be easy to do because of the circle you marked on it). Scoop out any moist pastry underneath. Place the cooked fish fillets and the mushrooms inside, replace the lid and keep warm.

Add the fish cooking liquor and the double cream to the *velouté* and reduce the sauce till it is thick enough to coat the back of a spoon. Add a little lemon juice and a pinch of cayenne pepper.

Take the lid off the pastry case, pour the sauce over the fish and mushrooms, replace the lid and serve at once. The rest of the bottle of dry cider you used for the sauce would be nice chilled and served with this.

SEAFOOD THERMIDOR

It would not be exaggerating to say that the success of our restaurant in our first ten years was due to this dish, which seemed to appeal to almost everyone. It had lots of different seafood in it, it was robustly flavoured, and it was the cheapest main course we sold. I still think it is a thoroughly delightful dish, even though I have given up serving it in the restaurant – mainly through boredom, but also because it is not at all fashionable at present. I shall revive it one day but until then here is the recipe for you to try.

4 oz (120 g) onion, finely chopped
2 oz (60 g) unsalted butter
3 fl oz (90 ml) dry white wine
10 fl oz (300 ml) fish stock
3 oz (90 g) fresh button mushrooms
20 fl oz (600 ml) velouté
4 fl oz (120 ml) double cream
6 oz (180 g) skinned lemon sole fillet
6 oz (180 g) skinned monkfish fillet
4 large scallops
4 oz (120 g) shelled North Atlantic prawns
1 tablespoon (15 ml) Colman's English mustard powder, made up with a little water
juice of a quarter lemon
3 oz (90 g) grated cheese

*1 oz (30 g) breadcrumbs
pinch of cayenne pepper*

Turn on your overhead grill. Soften the onion in the butter and pour in the white wine. Reduce a little, then add the fish stock and 1 oz (30 g) of the mushrooms. Simmer for 10 minutes, then reduce the volume by two-thirds by rapid boiling. Heat the *velouté* carefully and add the reduction to it (there is no need to strain this). Stir in the cream and leave simmering on a very low heat while you prepare the fish.

Cut the lemon sole and monkfish into ½-inch (1.2-cm) pieces. Slice each scallop into three. Put all the fish into a large shallow gratin dish. Sprinkle the rest of the mushrooms on top and brush with melted butter. Season with salt and place under the grill. Remove when the fish has turned white but is still a little underdone (it will cook more when you finish the dish by gratinating it under the grill). Now add the prawns to the rest of the fish. Add the mustard and lemon juice to the sauce and taste it; it should be slightly hot with mustard but not overpoweringly so. Pour the sauce over the fish and mushrooms. Mix the grated cheese with the breadcrumbs, the cayenne pepper and a couple of twists of the black pepper-mill and sprinkle over. Gratinate under the grill to a nice golden brown.

FISH CAKES WITH TURMERIC, CORIANDER AND CARDAMOM

The amount of spice in these fish cakes gives them a subtle flavour and an interesting colour but doesn'toverpower.

1 pint cider court bouillon
1½ lb (720 g) mackerel, herring or white fish
1 lb (450 g) floury potatoes, peeled and sliced
2 eggs
1 oz (30 g) butter
1 oz (30 g) chopped parsley
½ teaspoon (2.5 ml) ground turmeric
½ teaspoon (2.5 ml) coriander seeds
2 cardamoms
flour for coating hands
2 fl oz (60 ml) milk
2 oz (60 g) breadcrumbs
oil for shallow frying

Bring the *court bouillon* to the boil, add the fish and poach gently until just cooked. Remove the fish and cook the sliced potatoes in the *bouillon* till they are falling apart. Drain and mash the potato. Take the fillets off the fish, removing the skin. Beat one of the eggs into the potato with the butter and parsley.

Grind the turmeric, coriander and cardamom together in a grinder. Add the spices and the fish to the potato mixture and season.

Divide the mixture into eight and mould into flat cakes using floured hands. If the cakes are a bit soft, chill them for 30 minutes. Beat the remaining egg and add the milk. Coat the cakes in the egg mixture, then the breadcrumbs. Heat the oil in a frying pan and fry the fish cakes for 3 minutes on each side or until golden brown. Drain on kitchen paper.

Serve the fish cakes with a green salad dressed with walnut dressing and sprinkled with chopped coriander leaf.

HAKE AND POTATO PIE WITH A GARLIC, PARSLEY AND BREADCRUMB CRUST

1 lb (450 g) peeled potatoes
4 oz (120 g) butter
1 lb (450 g) skinned hake fillet
salt and freshly ground black pepper
2 slices of white bread
2 cloves of garlic
½ oz (15 g) parsley

Set your oven to 400°F (200°C; gas mark 6).

Cut the potato into ¼-inch (6-mm) slices. Parboil them in boiling salted water for 2 minutes. Smear half the butter round an oven dish; put the drained potato and the hake, cut into 1-inch (2.5-cm) slices, in it; season with salt and pepper and put the rest of the butter on top. Cover the dish and bake in the oven for 15 minutes, basting the fish and potatoes with the butter twice during that time.

Reduce the bread to crumbs in a food processor or liquidizer with the garlic and the parsley. Season the crumbs with a little salt and pepper.

Take the lid off the baking fish and potatoes and sprinkle with the breadcrumb mixture. Bake uncovered for a further 5 minutes or so till the top is crisp.

LEEK AND HAKE QUICHE

Fillets of hake with leeks cooked in butter in a light savoury custard flavoured with Noilly Prat and fish *fumet*.

> 8 oz (240 g) shortcrust pastry
> 3 oz (90 g) leek (outer leaves and top removed, well washed)
> ½ oz (15 g) butter
> ½ pint (300 ml) fish stock
> 1 fl oz (30 ml) Noilly Prat (or other dry vermouth)
> a little lemon juice and salt
> pinch of cayenne pepper
> 3 eggs
> 4 oz (120 ml) double cream
> 6 oz (180 g) hake fillet with skin removed

Preheat the oven to 375°F (190°C; gas mark 5).

You will need a deep 8-inch (20-cm) flan ring or flan case

for this dish. Roll out the pastry and line the flan case with it. Prick the pastry and cover it with greaseproof paper. Fill with baking beans. Bake for 10 minutes. Take out and remove beans and paper. Slice the leeks and soften them in the butter with a lid on the saucepan. Reduce the fish stock and Noilly Prat down to about 1 fl oz. (30 ml) by rapid boiling. Add the lemon juice, salt and cayenne pepper. Add this to the eggs and cream and beat together. Line the pastry case with the leeks. Cut the hake fillet into slices about the size of your little finger and lay these on top of the leeks. Pour the custard over and bake in the oven for 25 minutes.

BAKED PLAICE WITH CHEESE AND CIDER

This is a good dish to choose when you haven't much time, as it is quick to prepare and cook, and it tastes nice too.

2 oz (60 g) cheddar cheese
½ oz (15 g) butter
8 oz (240 g) onion
4 large fillets of plaice
salt and freshly ground black pepper
5 fl oz (150 ml) dry cider

Set the oven at 350°F (180°C; gas mark 4).

Grate the cheese. Melt the butter in a frying pan and fry the onions until soft. Transfer to a shallow baking dish. Place the fillets on top of the onions and season. Sprinkle with cheese, pour on the cider and bake in the centre of the oven for 20 minutes. I would serve this with mashed potatoes with a trace of garlic mashed up with a little salt and pepper mixed in. Some chilled dry cider would go well with it; I like the Breton or Normandy ciders which you can buy in England quite easily now. I also like the dry unfiltered cider of the Cornish Cider Company, Truro (tel. 01872 77177).

PLAICE AND ARTICHOKE PIE

The Jerusalem artichoke, when mashed half and half with potatoes, produces a purée with a sweet delicate flavour which goes very well with the plaice and the other vegetables in this pie. Serve it with cauliflower cooked *al dente* and then tossed in butter with some finely chopped onion.

1 lb (450 g) Jerusalem artichokes
1 lb (450 g) floury potatoes
3 oz (90 g) onion
4 oz (120 g) button mushrooms
1 lb (450 g) plaice fillet
a splash of dry cider
salt and ground black pepper
2 oz (60 g) butter
2 fl oz (60 ml) double cream

Set your oven to 400°F (200°C; gas mark 6).
Peel the artichokes and potatoes and cut them into pieces.

Bring to the boil in salted water and cook until soft. Peel and chop up the onion finely and slice the mushrooms. Butter a shallow oven-proof dish and sprinkle the onions over the bottom. Lay the mushrooms on the onions and put the plaice on top. Sprinkle with dry cider, lightly season with salt and ground black pepper and dot with a third of the butter.

Drain the artichokes and potatoes and mash them well. You may need to pass them through a sieve to get rid of the lumps in the artichoke; push it all through with the back of a large spoon.

Return the purée to the saucepan and heat gently while adding the cream and the remaining butter. Season to your taste and stir until it has stiffened up, then spread it over the fish and vegetables. Bake in the oven for 15–20 minutes until the top has browned nicely.

ESCALOPES OF SHARK WITH NOISETTE BUTTER

four 4-oz (120-g) escalopes of porbeagle shark
4 slices fresh white bread
6 fillets of anchovy
1 tablespoon (15 ml) chopped parsley
1 oz (30 g) flour
1 egg
1 tablespoon (15 ml) milk

1½ oz (45 g) butter
1½ oz (45 g) oil
4 oz (120 g) salted butter
juice of half a lemon
lemon wedges

The escalopes should be thin slices cut from a large piece of shark. They cannot be battered out like veal, since they break up, but it is fairly easy to get some reasonable slices from the middle. Alternatively you could use two thin slices per person from the tail, with the central cartilage removed. In both cases the thick skin should be cut off.

Turn the bread into crumbs in a food processor or liquidizer, adding the anchovy fillets and parsley at the same time. Put this in a shallow dish. Lightly beat the egg with the milk. Pass the escalopes first through the flour, then the egg mixture, and finally the breadcrumbs. Heat the butter and oil in a large frying pan and fry the escalopes to a nice golden brown. Do this in batches; don't overcrowd the pan. Pour out the butter and oil. Heat the 4 oz (120 g) of butter until it foams and smells nutty, then add the lemon juice and pour over the escalopes. Serve with extra wedges of lemon and some Parmentier potatoes. To go with this, I would like a bottle of DOC Soave, ice-cold and with that slightly bitter dryness some Italian wines have.

A *FRICASSÉE* OF SKATE WITH MUSHROOMS

Skate is normally but not always sold skinned. Skinning, unfortunately, is not particularly easy – one for the fishmonger if possible. For this recipe, you should buy good thick slabs of skate wing from a big fish; the smaller wings would take up too much room in the pan.

4 oz (120 g) fresh white mushrooms
1 teaspoon (5 ml) freshly chopped parsley
2 oz (60 g) butter
4 pieces of skinned skate each weighing about
  8 oz (240 g)
1 oz (30 g) flour
1 pint (600 ml) fish stock
1 egg yolk
2 fl oz (60 ml) double cream
juice of a quarter lemon

Thinly slice the mushrooms. Chop the parsley. Heat the butter in a sauté pan big enough to take all four fillets in a single layer. Put them in the pan, season with salt, cover with a lid and cook gently for 2 minutes on each side.

Add the flour and mix it in around the fish. Cook it for 2 minutes, then gradually add the fish stock. Bring to the boil and simmer till the fish is cooked through (about 20 minutes).

Remove the fillets with a perforated spoon and keep them warm in a serving dish. Simmer the sauce for a further

10 minutes and add any juice that has drained out of the fish. Add the mushrooms to the sauce and cook for a further 2 minutes. Remove from the heat.

Whisk the egg and cream together in a small bowl (this is called a liaison), then pour in a little of the boiling sauce. Stir the mixture back into the sauce. Do not reboil after this. Add the lemon juice and parsley, test the seasoning and pour over the skate. Serve with a green salad and boiled potatoes.

CHAR-GRILLED CONGER EEL WITH A RICH RED WINE SAUCE

The red wine sauce in this recipe could just as easily be served with steak, but it works well with these slightly charred fish steaks. They should ideally be cooked on a charcoal grill, but you can also achieve good results under a domestic grill.

four 8-oz (240-g) steaks of conger eel
1 teaspoon (5 ml) chopped fennel
2 bayleaves, sliced up
salt and black pepper
juice of a quarter lemon

For the Sauce

8 oz (240 g) onions, finely chopped
5 fl oz (150 ml) red wine

1 fl oz (30 ml) red wine vinegar
4 fl oz (120 ml) strong meat stock
½ teaspoon (2.5 ml) sugar
3 oz (90 g) unsalted butter

Put the conger steaks in a shallow dish with the fennel, bayleaves, salt, pepper and lemon juice. Leave to marinate for 30 minutes, turning occasionally.

Turn on your grill well in advance of cooking the steaks. If cooking over a charcoal fire, wait till the coals have just started to turn to ash before grilling the steaks.

Put the onions, red wine, red wine vinegar, stock and sugar in a sauteuse, bring to the boil and simmer gently till you have reduced the liquid right down to a thick juice with the onions.

Grill your steaks for about 5 minutes on each side; baste them by brushing a little of the marinade over them with a pastry brush. Test whether they are done by pushing the point of a small knife into the centre; the flesh should be white rather than translucent and should come away from the bones.

To finish off the sauce, cut the butter into a few lumps. Put the onion reduction back on to boil and whisk in the butter on the boil to form a shiny, viscous sauce. A simple green salad would go very well with this dish.

CASSOLETTE OF BRILL, SCALLOPS AND CRAB

Fish and shellfish cooked gently in a *cassolette* with the flavours of shellfish with tarragon and a little cream. A *cassolette* is a small round shallow copper pan. At the restaurant, this dish is cooked on top of the stove and served to the customer in the copper cooking pan. I have retained the name of the dish, because it sounds nice, but slightly changed the method to make it easier for you to cook at home.

>   *10 oz (360 g) skinned brill fillet*
>   *8 scallops*
>   *½ oz (15 g) butter*
>   *2 fl oz (60 ml) shellfish reduction*
>   *4 fl oz (120 ml) double cream*
>   *1 teaspoon (5 ml) fresh lemon juice*
>   *3 tomatoes, skinned, deseeded and chopped*
>   *1 teaspoon (5 ml) chopped tarragon*
>   *pinch cayenne pepper*
>   *8 oz (240 g) white crab meat*

Slice the brill into ½-inch (1.25-cm) pieces. Cut the scallops into three.

Select either a clean large non-stick or a thick-bottomed enamel frying pan (all-steel frying pans leave a metallic taste). Melt the butter in the pan; add the fish and a little later the scallops. Cook very gently in the butter.

As soon as the fish and scallops change from opaque to white, remove them to a warm plate with a fish slice. Add shellfish reduction and cream to the pan, turn up the heat and reduce the sauce until it is thick enough to coat the back of a spoon.

Add lemon juice, tomatoes, tarragon and cayenne. Return the fish and scallops to the pan and add the crab. Heat through, turning gently, and serve on four warm plates.

FILLETS OF BRILL *DUGLÉRÉ*

Brill is similar in taste and texture to turbot, and this good dish of classical French cuisine is pleasantly simple; the brill is poached in Muscadet with tomatoes and butter and served with a sauce made from the reduced poaching liquor and *velouté*. If you don't want to go to the trouble of making *velouté* you can substitute the same quantity of double cream, but this is one of those dishes which show how nice a *velouté*-based sauce can be.

1 oz (30 g) onion, finely chopped
3 good-sized tomatoes, skinned, deseeded and chopped
4 skinned fillets of brill, each weighing 6 oz (180 g)
3 fl oz (90 ml) Muscadet
salt and freshly ground white pepper
4 fl oz (120 ml) fish velouté
2 oz (60 g) unsalted butter

1 teaspoon (5 ml) chopped parsley
lemon juice
2 fl oz (60 ml) double cream

Turn on your oven to 350°F (180°C; gas mark 4).

Butter a shallow oven dish and sprinkle with the onion and tomato. Lay the fish fillets on top, add the Muscadet, and season lightly with salt and freshly ground white pepper (black pepper is a bit harsh for this recipe). Cover with a butter paper and poach in the oven for about 7–10 minutes.

Pour off the cooking liquor into a small pan and reduce it by half by rapid boiling. Add the fish *velouté*, butter, parsley and a few drops of lemon juice. Whisk to a smooth consistency, add the double cream, pour over the fish, *et voilà*, it's done.

POACHED HALIBUT STEAKS WITH HOLLANDAISE SAUCE

I like to bake steaks of fish in foil with a little liquid; in this way, the fish is poached in its own juices and no flavour is lost.

4 halibut steaks, each weighing 7 oz (175 g)
1 fl oz (30 ml) dry white wine
salt
about 8 oz (240 g) of the lightest hollandaise sauce

Set your oven to 375°F (190°C; gas mark 5).

Cut a piece of foil big enough to wrap up the halibut steaks easily, and butter one side of it. Season the steaks and place them side by side on the buttered foil. Splash with the white wine and wrap the steaks loosely, turning the two edges over a couple of times to make a good seal. Bake in the oven for 15 to 20 minutes. Open the parcel and place the steaks on a warm serving dish. Season them, pour the cooking juices over and serve with the hollandaise sauce.

MONKFISH COOKED LIKE A GIGOT OF LAMB WITH FENNEL AND GARLIC

Monkfish larded with slivers of garlic and pot-roasted in the oven with fennel, accompanied by a garlic sauce incorporating the roasting juice. This recipe describes the way we serve the fish in the restaurant, but you may find it more convenient to use one large monk tail, in which case buy one about 2½ lb (1.2 kg) and cook for about 45 minutes. For a special occasion, though, a whole tail each is a pleasant surprise, and as a reward for the extra work involved, small monk tails are cheaper than large ones.

POACHED SALMON WITH SAUCE VERTE

I prefer to poach salmon in salted water rather than in a *court bouillon*, because I don't think that fish as fine-flavoured as salmon needs anything added to it.

If you would prefer a *sauce verte* with a little more spice, use some coriander leaves as well as the ingredients below.

> *a piece of salmon weighing about 2½–3 lb*
>   *(1.2–1.4 kg)*
> *1 oz (30 g) spinach leaves*
> *1 oz (30 g) watercress*
> *1 oz (30 g) parsley, chervil, tarragon and chives*
>   *(in roughly equal quantities)*
> *½ pint (300 ml) olive oil mayonnaise*

Place the salmon in a fish kettle and pour on enough cold water to cover it. Add salt at the rate of 5 oz (150 g) to each gallon (5 litres). Bring the kettle to the boil, but then allow it to boil for only about 5 seconds. Remove it at once from the heat and let the salmon go quite cold in the water. This will produce a cooked salmon which is underdone and moist next to the bone.

Blanch all the green leaves in boiling water for one minute. Refresh in ice-cold water. Strain the herbs through a sieve, then squeeze them dry and liquidize them with a little of the mayonnaise. Mix in the rest of the mayonnaise and serve with the salmon.

Basics

FISH STOCK

1 large onion
1 large carrot
1 stick of celery, including the top
3 lb (1.4 kg) fish bones, including heads
3 pints (1.7 litres) water

Clean and peel the vegetables, then chop them into pieces roughly a quarter inch (6 mm) cube. The stock takes only 15 minutes to cook, so the vegetables must be cut small to extract the maximum flavour in so short a cooking time. Place the vegetables in a large saucepan (holding at least 6 pints or 3 litres) and put the fish trimmings on top. Pour on the water and bring slowly to the boil. As soon as the stock comes to the boil, turn the heat right down and leave at a very slow simmer for 15 minutes. Take the pan off the heat and leave the stock to go quite cold before straining. Making stock this way keeps the liquor clear and clean-tasting.

ROUILLE

The fiery accompaniment to fish soup and *bouillabaisse*. If you are in a hurry, you can just mix mayonnaise with garlic and cayenne pepper. But here is the recipe we use in the restaurant, which needs *harissa*, a chilli, red pepper and coriander sauce from North Africa. It is available in small tins from good continental food shops, but we have evolved our own recipe, which seems about right.

Harissa

1 tablespoon (15 ml) tomato purée
1 tablespoon (15 ml) ground coriander
1 teaspoon (5 ml) powdered saffron
3 red peppers, deseeded, roasted and skinned
15 green chillies (small hot)
1 teaspoon (5 ml) salt
1 teaspoon (5 ml) cayenne pepper

Put all the ingredients in a liquidizer and blend.

Rouille

2 oz (60 g) dry bread, soaked in fish stock
6 cloves garlic
1 egg yolk

6 tablespoons (90 ml) harissa
½ teaspoon (2.5 ml) salt
¾ pint (450 ml) olive oil

Put all the ingredients except the olive oil in a food processor and blend. Then pour in the oil as for making mayonnaise.

CLEANING MUSSELS

Disregard any information about leaving mussels in a bucket of cold water to let them cleanse themselves (with or without a handful of oatmeal). Mussels are extremely particular about the type of water they find themselves in. A bucket of cold tap water will cause them to stay firmly closed, since they very quickly sense that there is no air in the water and that it is not salty. They will not self-cleanse unless they are in seawater or brackish water which is well aerated. Furthermore, leaving them for any length of time in a bucket of still water will soon kill them. There is in any case no need to clean mussels like this, because unlike cockles, which live under sand, they are not gritty.

Wash mussels in the sink with plenty of changes of cold water, swirling them round and round each time until the water is clear. Scrape the mussels with a short thick-bladed knife to remove any barnacles or seaweed, and pull out the beards if you are going to serve them as *moules marinières* or in any other dish where they are cooked and served immediately. (If you are going on to stuff them, it is easier to remove the beards after you have cooked them and let them cool down.)

VELOUTÉ

In the best culinary circles, flour-based sauces are frowned on nowadays as belonging to the old stodgy school of cookery rather than the *nouvelle*, or perhaps *moderne*, lighter approach. The new method is to thicken a sauce with a lot of butter and cream and air rather than a roux, and at their best these sauces are excellent balancing acts between lightness and extreme richness; at their worst, the excess of fat blankets any taste.

A well-made *velouté*-based sauce certainly shouldn't taste heavy or floury. As its name implies, it should taste velvety and carry no suggestion of the flour that went into it. To achieve the right texture the flour must be thoroughly cooked by long low simmering.

TO MAKE ONE PINT (600 ML)

1 pint (600 ml) of fish stock
2 oz (60 g) butter
1½ oz (45 g) flour

Bring the fish stock to the boil. Meanwhile melt the butter in a second, thick-bottomed pan, add the flour and cook for about 2 minutes, stirring constantly. Don't let the roux colour too much. When it starts to smell nutty, remove from the heat and cool a little. Gradually add the hot stock, stirring all the time until smooth, then return to the heat. Turn the heat right down and simmer for about 40 minutes, stirring occasionally to prevent the bottom sticking. Pass the sauce through a conical strainer into a bowl, cover with a butter paper to prevent a skin forming, and if not using immediately, chill when cooled.

AÏOLI

8 cloves of garlic
2 egg yolks
juice of a quarter lemon
a pinch of salt
12 fl oz (360 ml) of a good first-pressing olive oil
  (usually called virgin)

IF MAKING WITH A MORTAR AND PESTLE: Reduce the garlic to a purée with the pestle, add the salt, egg yolks and lemon juice, and beat in the oil in a steady drizzle.

IF MAKING IN A FOOD PROCESSOR: Put the garlic, egg yolks and lemon juice in the food processor. Turn it on and blend it for about 10 seconds, then add the oil slowly to build up a thick mayonnaise.